Alexander Graham Bell

History Maker Bios

Stephanie Sammartino McPherson

LERNER PUBLICATIONS COMPANY • MINNEAPOLIS

For Marianne, my inventive, creative, inspiring daughter

Note on Spelling: Until his marriage, Alexander Graham Bell spelled his nickname Aleck. After he became engaged to Mabel Hubbard, she asked him to drop the final *K*. Bell agreed and began writing his nickname as Alec. To avoid confusion, this is the spelling used throughout this book.

Illustrations by Tad Butler

Text copyright © 2007 by Stephanie Sammartino McPherson
Illustrations copyright © 2007 by Lerner Publishing Group, Inc.

Lerner Publications Company
A division of Lerner Publishing Group, Inc.
241 First Avenue North
Minneapolis, MN 55401 U.S.A.

Website address: www.lernerbooks.com

Library of Congress Cataloging-in-Publication Data

McPherson, Stephanie Sammartino.
    Alexander Graham Bell / by Stephanie Sammartino McPherson; illustrations by Tad Butler.
        p.   cm. — (History maker bios)
    Includes bibliographical references and index.
    ISBN-13: 978–0–8225–7606–8 (lib. bdg. : alk. paper)
    1. Bell, Alexander Graham, 1847–1922—Juvenile literature. 2. Inventors—United States—Biography—Juvenile literature. I. Butler, Tad. II. Title.
    TK6143.B4M39 2007
    621.385092—dc22 [B]   2006037732

Manufactured in the United States of America
1 2 3 4 5 6 – JR – 12 11 10 09 08 07

TABLE OF CONTENTS

INTRODUCTION

Alexander Graham Bell wanted to know everything about sound. How was it made? How did the human voice work? One thing interested him most of all. Could voices travel over electric wires? Bell proved that they could. That meant that people far apart would be able to talk with one another. Bell invented the telephone and changed the world forever.

But the telephone was only the beginning. Bell also invented a metal detector and a breathing machine. He built giant kites and flying machines. And he designed special boats. They seemed to fly just above the water. Alexander Graham Bell was so full of ideas that sometimes he would feel them "tingling to [his] fingertips."

This is his story.

YOUNG INVENTOR

Alexander Bell was born on March 3, 1847, in the city of Edinburgh, Scotland. Eliza and Alexander Melville Bell nicknamed their son Alec. Young Alec liked adventure. When he was very small, his parents took him on a picnic. Alec got lost in a field of tall wheat. He was trying to hear the wheat grow!

Even Alec's sharp ears could not hear the wheat. But at night, he lay in bed listening to dogs bark. He could tell which neighbor's dog was barking. He could also tell which church bells were chiming.

Alec had an older brother, Melville (Melly), and a younger brother, Edward (Ted). They liked sounds too. Often the three brothers made animal sounds to show off for visitors. They also put on puppet shows.

The Bell family enjoyed picnics in their garden. Their house was named Milton Cottage.

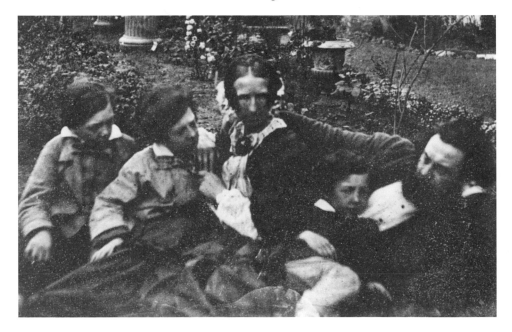

But Alec's best talent was playing the piano. He didn't need to read the music. All he needed to do was hear a song. Then he could play it by ear. Alec was sure he would grow up to be a musician.

Alec's parents were happy that he loved music. Melville Bell was a speech teacher. He helped people overcome problems such as stuttering. Alec's mother was deaf, but she was a pianist too. When Alec played, she could feel the way the piano quivered with the music.

Alexander Melville Bell (LEFT) taught at the University of Edinburgh. Eliza Bell (RIGHT) was a painter and musician.

Farmers raise grain crops, as well as cows and sheep, on the rolling hills around Edinburgh.

Alec and his mother were very close. Until Alec was ten years old, Eliza taught him at home. After that, Alec attended school. But he would rather spend time at his family's cottage in the country than sit in class. Roaming the fields, Alec collected plants, birds' eggs, and bugs.

Alec also liked to visit a nearby flour mill. The mill belonged to the father of one of his friends, Ben Herdman. One day, Alec and Ben were fooling around. "Why don't you do something useful?" Ben's father asked. He said they should find a way to remove the husks from grains of wheat.

Stalks of freshly harvested wheat (RIGHT) must have the hard, pointy husks removed from wheat kernels (MIDDLE). The kernels are then ground into flour (LEFT).

The husk is the hard shell around the soft center of the wheat. This center is called the kernel. Husks had to be removed before the kernels could be made into flour. It was a slow job.

Alec thought of a machine he had seen in the barn. The machine had paddles that spun around. Alec added brushes to the machine. The brushes and paddles scraped the husks off the wheat. Mr. Herdman was amazed. This was Alec's first invention.

At the age of fourteen, Alec graduated from Edinburgh's Royal High School. Then he went to stay with his grandfather in London for a year. Grandfather Bell made Alec read more and dress in fancier clothes. His grandfather gave him more freedom than he had at home. Later, Alec said that he turned from a boy into a man while staying with his grandfather.

Alec had his picture taken when he graduated from high school. He was fourteen years old.

Before Alec left London, his father took him to see a scientist named Charles Wheatstone. Wheatstone showed them a machine he had made. The machine sounded out a few easy words.

Back home in Edinburgh, Alec's father suggested that Alec and Melly make a talking machine of their own. Such a machine would be a teaching tool. It would show the boys how the human voice worked.

Charles Wheatstone experimented with sending messages over electrical wires. He also invented a musical instrument called a concertina.

Alec and Melly went right to work. They built a talking machine out of rubber and part of an organ. When their machine was done, it looked like a big head. The boys tested it on the stairs outside the Bell house. "Mama!" squealed the invention. One neighbor thought that a baby was crying. Alec and Melly were delighted. They never explained that the "baby" was only a machine!

Choosing a Name

When Alec was eleven, he decided he needed a fancier name. His father and grandfather were both Alexander Bell. Alec borrowed his middle name from a man named Alexander Graham, who was visiting Alec's family. The name stuck. From then on, he was Alexander Graham Bell.

2 GREAT IDEA

Alec wanted more excitement in his life. For a while, he thought about running away to sea. Instead, he became a teacher at a boys' school in Elgin. This city is in northeast Scotland. Alec taught music and speech. He was only sixteen years old. Some of his students were older than he was!

Alec took some time off to attend the University of Edinburgh. But he was more interested in studying human speech on his own. He also became interested in his father's new alphabet. Melville had created symbols for every sound that human beings could make. The special alphabet showed speakers how to say words in any language. He called it visible speech.

VISIBLE SPEECH

Alec and his brothers helped their father put on shows about visible speech. While the brothers were in another room, Melville gathered words from people in the audience. Some words were in foreign languages, such as Persian or Sanskrit, that his sons had never heard. Melville Bell wrote the words on a blackboard with his visible speech symbols. Then the boys returned to the room. They were able to look at the board and say the words perfectly.

[ENGLISH ALPHABET OF VISIBLE SPEECH,
Expressed in the Names of Numbers and Objects.]

[Pronounce the Nos.]	[Names.]	[Name the Objects.]		[Name the Objects.]	
1.					
2.					
3.					
4.					
5.					
6.					
7.					
8.					

Visible speech used symbols to spell out the sounds of words.

[EXERCISE.]

One by one.
Two or three.
Four at once.
Five o'clock.
Half-past six.
Seven-thirty.
Eight to nine.
Ten or twelve.
Twice two, four.
Twice three, six.
Four and four, eight.
Nine and two, eleven.

Two, a couple.
Twelve, a dozen.
Twenty, a score.
A book-case.
A few books.
New book-shelves.
A silver watch.
A gold watch.
The watch-key.
A good saw.
Cap and feather.
Tongs and shovel.

A hunting whip.
A table lamp.
A bunch of onions.
Corns and bunions.
A ship's boat.
A sailing boat.
Cart and horse.
A round tent.
Rows of houses.
A dog-kennel.
A little monkey.
A pretty cane.

When Alec was twenty years old, his brother Ted died of a lung disease called tuberculosis. Three years later, his older brother, Melly, died of the same illness. The family was heartbroken.

Alec's parents worried about the health of their only remaining child. Alec suffered from headaches and sleeplessness. His parents thought that the fresh air and open spaces of Canada would be better for him. They decided to move.

16

At first, twenty-three-year-old Alec didn't like Canada. He missed the rush of big city life. But Alec's health improved. He roamed the countryside and made friends with a Mohawk Indian chief named George Johnson. George taught Alec a foot-stomping war dance. Alec loved it.

With his father's help, Alec got a job in Boston, Massachusetts. Alec taught deaf children. He showed his students how to use their tongues and lips and vocal cords to make sounds. Then he helped them speak properly by teaching them his father's alphabet.

Alec (TOP ROW RIGHT) poses with his students at the Boston School for the Deaf.

Science also fascinated Alec. He went to science lectures nearby at the famous Massachusetts Institute of Technology. He read everything he could find about electricity. Soon he became interested in the telegraph. Telegraph machines sent coded messages over electric wires. The person who received the message heard a series of beeps and clicks. These were used to spell out words. The first telegraphs could only send one message at a time.

Early telegraph users typed out coded messages on machines like this.

Alec gave speech lessons in his home. He taught deaf students to make the word sounds that they could not hear.

Alec learned that inventors were trying to make a telegraph that could send more than one message at a time. This sounded like a good idea to him. In 1872, twenty-five-year-old Alec began his own experiments. He wanted to be the one to invent the new kind of telegraph. He called it the harmonic telegraph.

Alec's experiments began to take over his life. During the day, he taught deaf students at his lodgings. At night, Alec lost track of time as he worked on the telegraph. Often he forgot to eat. His health suffered, but his mind crackled with ideas.

Alec's parents lived in this house near the Grand River.

Alec wanted to do more than send a series of beeps from one place to another. He believed it was possible to send any sound over electric wires. That included human speech. Instead of using the telegraph, people could actually speak to each other over the electric wires!

In June 1874, Alec returned to Canada to spend summer vacation with his parents. Alec had a favorite spot overlooking the Grand River. He called it his dreaming place. Alec was sitting in his dreaming place one day when he had an exciting idea about what he had begun to call the telephone.

Every sound creates small movements in the air around it. These patterns are called vibrations. Alec wanted to change the flow of electricity to match a sound's vibrations. Then he should be able to send any sound from one place to another. Eagerly, he drew a sketch of what he had in mind.

Alec knew he faced many problems. He had studied hard, but he didn't know as much about electricity as scientists did. And he didn't have enough money to pay for more equipment. Could Alec turn his idea into a real invention? He could only hope so.

Alec filled many notebooks with sketches of his inventions. He drew this sketch of his telephone in 1876.

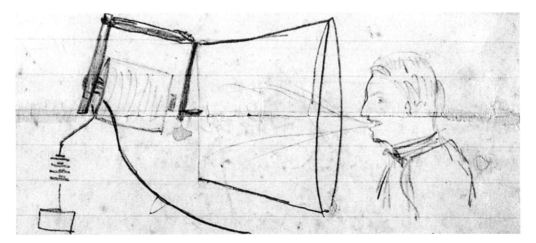

3 "THIS THING SPEAKS!"

Alec became a speech professor at Boston University. He also taught deaf students privately. One Sunday afternoon, he went to tea at the home of Mabel Hubbard, one of his students. Alec told her family about his work on the telephone. Mabel's father, Gardiner Hubbard, was impressed. He offered to help Alec financially.

Alec was already receiving money from the father of another deaf pupil, George Sanders. At last, Alec had the funds to keep working. But he still needed another kind of help. Alec had always been clumsy with tools. Someone would have to help him put together his equipment. Luckily, Alec met Thomas Watson at an electrical workshop. Watson made some electrical equipment for Alec. He was good with tools and knew a lot about electricity.

Alec and Watson worked on the telephone in this laboratory in Boston.

On June 2, 1875, Alec and Thomas Watson were working together. They were in separate rooms. Alec expected to hear the usual clicks that a telegraph made. Instead, he heard a twang. Alec yelled with excitement. He rushed to see what Watson was doing. Watson had only plucked a strip of metal. But the sound had changed the electric current as Alec had said it would. From that moment, Alec knew that sounds other than clicks could be sent over a wire. He had proof that his idea would work.

Fateful Meeting

Joseph Henry of the Smithsonian Institution was one of the country's leading experts on electricity. In 1875, Alec visited Henry. He told Henry about his idea for the telephone. "You have the germ of a great invention. Work at it," said Henry. When Alec worried that he didn't have enough knowledge of electricity, Henry replied, "Get it!" Later, Alec wrote, "But for Joseph Henry, I should never have gone on with the telephone."

Mabel (RIGHT) was one of Alec's deaf students. When she was five, she lost her hearing to a disease called scarlet fever.

Something else important happened to Alec. He fell in love with Mabel Hubbard. Alec was twenty-eight. Mabel was only seventeen. Although she respected her teacher, Mabel didn't think she could return his feelings.

Alec's love and kindness won Mabel over. On her eighteenth birthday, November 25, 1875, Alec and Mabel became engaged. Alec had a new reason to complete work on his telephone. He hoped it would make enough money for him to support a wife.

Neither of Alec's financial backers thought he would make much money from the telephone. They thought it was just an interesting toy. But just in case he was wrong, Gardiner Hubbard filed a patent application at the U.S. Patent Office in Washington, D.C., on February 14, 1876.

A patent would protect Alec's ideas. It would show that he came up with the idea first, before anyone else. Anyone who wanted to use Alec's work would have to pay him. Alec had a very special birthday present that year. His patent was granted.

But Alec still hadn't sent any words over the telephone. One week after getting his patent, he was working with Watson again. The two men were in separate rooms. Watson had his ear pressed to the telephone. To his shock, he heard the words, "Mr. Watson, come here. I want you!" Alec and Watson were thrilled.

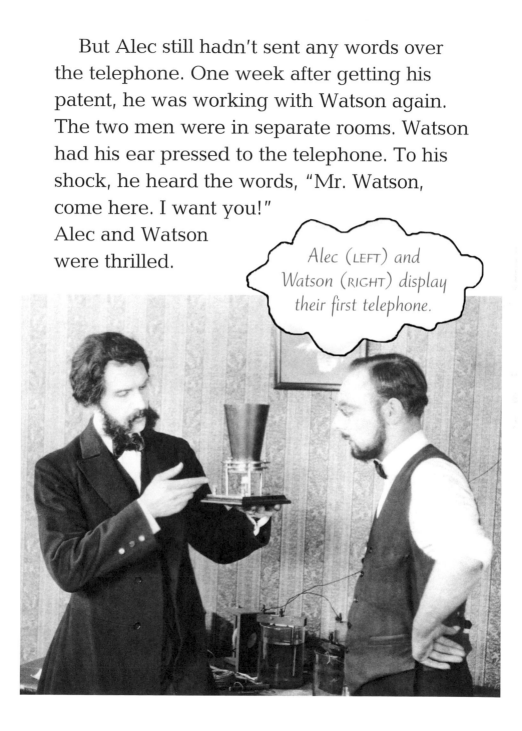

Alec (LEFT) and Watson (RIGHT) display their first telephone.

Alec (CENTER) explains his telephone to scientists (RIGHT) and an audience of curious people from Salem, Massachusetts.

Alec felt ready to show his invention to other scientists. He took the telephone to important science conferences. Mabel even talked him into taking the telephone to the one-hundredth birthday celebration of the United States. The fair took place in Philadelphia, Pennsylvania. It had many exhibits. Alec entered the telephone in a contest for electric inventions. The judges were hot and tired. They almost missed Alec's telephone. But Dom Pedro, the emperor of Brazil, was also at the exhibit.

Dom Pedro had met Alec at a school for the deaf in Boston. When the emperor greeted Alec, the judges took note. They wanted to see what the emperor's friend had invented.

Dom Pedro was the first person at the fair to hear Alec's words over the telephone. "This thing speaks!" he cried. The judges were amazed. They awarded Alec a gold medal.

Dom Pedro II, emperor of Brazil, wanted his own country to have exciting new inventions like the telephone.

Alec continued to work on his invention. So far, he had only made one-way calls. This was because different telephones were needed for speaking and listening. He could only call out on one kind of telephone. He could only listen on another kind. In the fall, Alec decided to try a two-way call. He stayed in Boston. Watson took a telephone for listening and another for speaking to Cambridge, Massachusetts. The two men heard each other fine. Later that night, they celebrated. Yelling loudly, they broke into an Indian war dance.

4 FAMOUS INVENTOR

Alec decided to make money by putting on telephone shows. First, he would hire a public hall. Then he set Watson up with a telephone somewhere else. The audience could scarcely believe what Alec said about the telephone. Then they heard Watson singing and speaking from twenty miles away. People cheered.

Alec used part of his earnings to buy Mabel a silver model of a telephone. On July 11, 1877, they were married. Several weeks later, the happy couple set off for a trip to Great Britain. Already more than two hundred telephones were being used in the United States. And the number was rising rapidly.

RING! RINGGGG!

Before 1877, telephones did not ring. Anyone making a call shouted into the telephone in hope that someone at the other end would hear. Of course, this system meant a lot of missed calls. Then Tom Watson invented a special ringer. People could hear the bells even if they weren't standing right by the telephone. Watson went on to make many improvements to the telephone.

Alec spent a lot of time showing off the telephone in Great Britain. He sent a telephone into a coal mine so the miners could be heard aboveground. He also put on a diving suit and was lowered into the Thames River. Alec set up a telephone connection between the divers underwater and the people on the surface. Even Queen Victoria asked for a demonstration of the telephone.

After several months, the Bells were eager to return to the United States. But Mabel was expecting a baby. The doctor did not think she should make the long ocean trip.

On May 10, 1878, Elsie May was born in London, England. By the time Alec, Mabel, and baby Elsie set sail for home, Alec was having legal problems. Two inventors, Elisha Gray and Thomas Edison, had done their own work on the telephone. Gray and Edison worked with the Western Union Company. The company was ignoring Alec's patent. It made and sold telephones without paying him anything. Mabel's father, Gardiner Hubbard, filed a lawsuit to stop the company.

Thomas Edison displays his phonograph. He also invented a new kind of lightbulb and an early movie camera called a kinetoscope.

The apparatus was made specially for the occasion and worked well.

A ... M ... Z

Battery

S and S' are pieces of steel spring about the size of...

This sketch helped to prove that Alec was the first to have the idea for the telephone.

Alec hated to be involved in the lawsuit. But he would lose a great deal of money if he did not defend his patent. There were already thousands of telephones across the United States. Alec used his records to prove he had been the first to invent the telephone. He gave convincing testimony in the courtroom.

The Western Union lawyer decided that they couldn't beat Alec after all. They agreed to stay out of the telephone business. Through the years, six hundred lawsuits involving the telephone went to court. Alec won every case.

The photophone (ABOVE) used light to send sound. Alec wanted to send messages without using wires.

The telephone made Alec rich. But Alec was getting tired of the telephone. He had so many ideas. One idea was to use light rays to carry sound waves through the air. Then no wires would be needed to send a message. Alec invented a device he called the photophone. He sent sound through the air without wires.

That same week, Mabel gave birth to a daughter on February 15, 1880. Alec considered naming her Photophone! But Mabel put her foot down. They named the little girl Marian but called her Daisy.

Several months later, Alec received an important award from the French government. France wanted to honor Alec for inventing the telephone. By this time, the Bells had moved to Washington, D.C. Alec used his prize money to buy a house in the city. He also set up a small science lab. He was determined to be known for more than the telephone.

Alec bought this large house on Connecticut Avenue in Washington, D.C., for his growing family.

5 "A HUNDRED DIFFERENT DIRECTIONS"

In July 1881, a national emergency set Alec to work on another invention. President James Garfield had been shot. Alec invented a metal detector to try to locate the bullet. The device didn't work for Garfield. The president died. But the metal detector proved useful in several wars. It helped doctors find bullets in wounded men.

Alec suffered a personal tragedy during this time. His third child, a little boy, was born with breathing problems. The baby died a few hours after birth. Alec handled his grief by working on another invention. He designed a metal jacket for people too weak to breathe on their own. The jacket pushed air in and out of a patient's lungs.

Alec was so caught up in his big ideas that sometimes he forgot to sleep. He stayed up half the night working or playing the piano. Mabel got Alec up in the mornings and watched over his health. She took care of all the details—such as paying the bills—that Alec wouldn't bother with. But Mabel didn't mind. Alec and Mabel had a happy marriage.

Alec made sketches of his inventions. This sketch shows a machine to help people who can't breathe on their own.

The Bell mansion in Nova Scotia had a laboratory, workshops, an observatory, and a tennis court.

On November 10, 1882, Alec became a U.S. citizen. Three years later, he took Mabel and their children on a summer trip to Nova Scotia, Canada. The family especially enjoyed the small town of Baddeck. Every summer, the family returned. Little by little, Alec bought land near the town. It was so lovely that he gave it the Scots name Beinn Bhreagh. This means "beautiful mountain."

Alec built a big house on his land. When it was finished in 1892, a newspaper called it "the finest mansion in eastern Canada." Alec was happier in Canada than anywhere else. He spent hours watching eagles soar.

The eagles made Alec think about flying machines. Ever since he was a boy, Alec had been fascinated with the idea of human flight. He thought he could learn about human flight by watching kites fly.

Over time, Alec's interest in flying increased. He formed a group to test and design biplanes. These airplanes have two wings on each side, one on top of the other. Alec called these planes "aerodromes." The Wright brothers were the first to fly a true airplane in 1903. But in 1909, a member of Alec's group made the first airplane flight in Canada.

Alec tests a kite made in the shape of a tetrahedron. Tetrahedrons are light but strong.

Boats also interested Alec. He designed special boats called hydrofoils. The boats had long, flat blades that stuck out from both sides. These foils acted as underwater wings. They pushed the boat up so it seemed to fly along the top of the water. In 1919, one of Alec's hydrofoils set a speed record of seventy-one miles per hour. That made it the fastest boat in the world!

COAST-TO-COAST

In 1915, a ceremony was held in honor of the first telephone line to cross the country. Alec and Tom Watson made the first coast-to-coast call. Alec was on the East Coast. Tom was on the West Coast. "Hoy! Hoy!" said Alec. It was the way he always said hello. Remembering the first telephone message, Alec continued, "Mr. Watson, come here. I want you." Tom replied that they were so far apart that it would take a week rather than a minute to get to Alec.

The wide fields and open water near Beinn Bhreagh were perfect for Alec's experiments with boats and kites (ABOVE).

As Alec grew older, he still longed for adventure. He became interested in solar power and recycling. He even predicted that one day people would send letters to each other by using electricity. To Mabel, it seemed that he was going in "a hundred different directions."

Alec's body could not keep pace with his active mind. He had diabetes, a disease that can lead to heart attack and stroke. Alec died on August 2, 1922. The day of his funeral, all telephone service was stopped for one minute in remembrance of him. Although many of Alec's ideas were ahead of their time, they lived on to help shape the modern world.

TIMELINE

ALEXANDER GRAHAM BELL
WAS BORN ON
MARCH 3, 1847.

In the year . . .

1863   Alec became a teacher in Elgin, Scotland.

1870   he moved to Canada with his parents.   Age 23

1871   he began teaching deaf children in Boston.

1872   he began his experiments with the telegraph.

1874   he sketched out his plans for the telephone.

1875   he heard a twang over telegraph lines.
he became engaged to Mabel Hubbard.

1876   his telephone patent was granted.   Age 29
he transmitted words over electric wires.
he won a gold medal at the U.S. centennial
celebration.
he made the first two-way call.

1877   he married Mabel Hubbard on July 11.

1878   his daughter Elsie May was born on May 10.
he became involved in a series of lawsuits
about telephone patents.

1880   he invented the photophone.   Age 33
his daughter Marian "Daisy" was born on
February 15.
he received the Volta Prize from the French
government.

1881   he invented a metal detector and a metal
breathing jacket.

1882   he became a U.S. citizen.

1892   his house in Baddeck, Nova Scotia, was
completed.

1898   he became president of the National   Age 51
Geographic Society.

1919   his hydrofoil set a world speed record.

1922   he died on August 2.   Age 75

"THE WORLD AND ALL THAT'S IN IT"

Alec's father-in-law had a great idea. He wanted to spread knowledge. Alec agreed to help. Thirty-three other men joined them to form the National Geographic Society *(below)*. They published a small magazine. But few people read it. Most of the articles were difficult.

When Alec became the president of the National Geographic Society in 1898, he made big changes. He wanted lots of people to read the magazine. Alec came up with a new slogan for the magazine, "The world and all that's in it." He hoped that it would attract readers.

Alec hired a young man, Gilbert Grosvenor, to edit the magazine. Alec wanted lots of photographs. They should be full of "life and action," he declared. They should be "pictures that tell a story." One year later, twice as many subscribers received the magazine. *National Geographic* became one of the most popular and respected magazines in the country.

FURTHER READING

Pfeffer, Wendy. *Sound All Around.* **New York: HarperCollins Publishers, 1999.** This book explains what sound is and explores different kinds of sounds in the world.

Sherrow, Victoria. *Alexander Graham Bell.* **Minneapolis: Lerner Publications Company, 2001.** This biography of Bell tells the story of the invention of the telephone and features full-page illustrations.

Zemlica, Shannon. *Thomas Edison.* **Minneapolis: Lerner Publications Company, 2004.** The story of another great inventor—the man who invented the electric lightbulb and tried to beat Bell in the race to invent the telephone.

WEBSITES

Alexander Graham Bell Family Collection—The Kids Zone
http://bell.uccb.ns.ca/kidsindex.asp This website allows you to click on experiments that Alexander Graham Bell designed especially for children.

AT&T Labs for Fun: Who Was Alexander Graham Bell?
http://www.att.com/attlabs/technology/forfun/alexbell/
This website has information on Bell as a teacher, a tinkerer, and an inventor. There is also a matching activity.

The Federal Communications Commission (FCC) Kids Zone–History of the Telephone
http://www.fcc.gov/kidszone/history_telephone.html This website explains how Bell invented the telephone.

Number Please: Connect with the First Telephone Operators
http://pbskids.org/wayback/tech1900/phone.html Learn fun facts about the first telephone operators.

SELECT BIBLIOGRAPHY

Bruce, Robert V. "Alexander Graham Bell," *National Geographic*, September 1988, 358–385.

Bruce, Robert V. *Bell: Alexander Graham Bell and the Conquest of Solitude*. Boston: Little, Brown and Company, 1973.

Eber, Dorothy Harley. *Genius at Work: Images of Alexander Graham Bell*. Halifax, NS: Nimbus Publishing, 1991.

Gray, Charlotte. *Reluctant Genius: Alexander Graham Bell and the Passion for Invention*. New York: Arcade Publishing, 2006.

Grosvenor, Edwin S., and Morgan Wesson. *Alexander Graham Bell: The Life and Times of the Man Who Invented the Telephone*. New York: Harry N. Abrams, 1997.

Matthews, Tom L. *Always Inventing: A Photobiography of Alexander Graham Bell*. Washington, DC: National Geographic Society, 1999.

Pasachoff, Naomi. *Alexander Graham Bell: Making Connections*. New York: Oxford University Press, 1996.

PBS. "The American Experience/The Telephone/Program Transcript." PBS /WGBH. 2000. http://www.pbs.org/wgbh/amex/telephone/filmmore/transcript/index.html (January 30, 2007).

INDEX

Acknowledgments

For photographs and artwork: © North Wind Picture Archives, p. 4; Library of Congress, pp. 7 (LC-G9-Z10-31), 8 left (LC-G9-Z1-155,874-A-2), 11 (LC-G9-Z1-14,503-A-1), 16 (LC-USZ62-104427), 20 (LC-G9-Z2-12494-B), 21, 26, 29 (LC-USZ62-74644), 34 (LC-DIG-cwpbh-04044), 35, 39, 41, 43; © SSPL/The Image Works, p. 8 (right); © David Lyons/Alamy, p. 9; © Mauritius/SuperStock, p. 10; © NMPFT/SSPL/The Image Works, p. 12; © Time & Life Pictures/Getty Images, pp. 17, 23, 33; © Bettmann/CORBIS, pp. 18, 19; The Granger Collection, New York, p. 25; © CORBIS, pp. 27, 37; © Getty Images, p. 28; © Mary Evans Picture Library/Alamy, p. 36; © Visions of America, LLC/Alamy, p. 40; © Underwood & Underwood/CORBIS, p. 45.

Front Cover: © John M. Daugherty/Photo Researchers, Inc.
Back Cover: Library of Congress (LC-D420-2586)

For quoted material: pp. 5, 29, 40, 43, Charlotte Gray, *Reluctant Genius: Alexander Graham Bell and the Passion for Invention* (New York: Arcade Publishing, 2006); p. 9, Robert V. Bruce, *Bell: Alexander Graham Bell and the Conquest of Solitude* (Boston: Little, Brown and Company, 1973); pp. 24, 27, 42, Naomi Pasachoff, *Alexander Graham Bell: Making Connections* (New York: Oxford University Press, 1996).